AN APOLOGY GONE WRONG

Pamela Knight Copyright © 2018 Pamela Knight

All rights reserved

SURVIVORS

If you have been abused or currently a victim of abuse and have not yet spoken out. I urge you to reach toward a safe person and speak your truth. You too are strong and courageous and deserve to live an abuse free life. Stand with me, no longer a victim but a survivor.

CONTENTS

1	An Apology Gone Wrong
1	Purpose of Life
2	My Love of Writing God Picked Out for Me
3	Love Is Love
4	My Dream of Writing Just as I Write God Picked Out For Me
5	My Dream of Writing Conversations Allow You to Adopt A Role
6	Reading Have Purposes, Needs, Interest, Knowledge And Backgrounds
7	Writing Conversations Help Share Ideas, and Arguments
8	Attractions
9	Faith
10	Tests and Trials
11	Strong
12	Love, Family and Forgiveness
13	What the Bible Say About Favoritism
14	The Parenting Perils of Favoritism
15	Secrets
16	Inside Out Change Starts Within
17	Survivor
18	How Parents Create Sibling Rivalry
19	Strangers We Call Family

Forgiveness

As those who have been chosen of God, holy and beloved, put on a heart of compassion... bearing with one another, forgiving each other, whosoever has a complaint against anyone: just as the Lord forgave you, so also should you. Col 3: 12-13   Unforgiveness holds us hostage, and when we find ourselves prisoners of what someone else has done to us or perhaps what we have done to ourselves.

Forgiveness does not mean approving a wrong or excusing an evil. Forgiveness isn't necessarily the reconciliation of the relationship. Forgiveness is our choice to release a person from obligation for a wrong committed against us. God says to forgive one another because he paid the greatest price-the price of our sin debt-with his own son. Loving God, loving others is the greatest commandment. Jesus showed us great compassion as he gave his life for us.

Dear Lord, Thank You for the unique way that you have gifted me. Help me to use my gifts faithfully to serve you and others, each person is a unique expression of God's loving design.

ACKNOWLEDGMENTS

Acknowledgments and copyrights are continued at the back of the book, which constitute an extension of the copyright page. It is a violation of the law to reproduce these selections by any means whatsoever without the written permission of the copyright holder.

1 An Apology Gone Wrong

"An Apology Gone Wrong" Just as I write God out for message for anyone who's been abused. "No one can go back and start a new beginning, but you can start today and make a new end I was five years old an only child in 1965. my mother and father were not married, went their separate ways. It was a long time before I saw my dad again.

I was almost finishing high school when my dad came to pick me up and visit with him. _Pamela Knight #Its on Us, Me Too.

My step father molested me from five years, old to fourteen years old. He would wait until my mother was never at home or if she was asleep. I would began telling my mother at the age of five until I was fourteen years. My step father would come in my room while I was asleep and touch me inappropriately. He would put his fingers in my private parts and he had long fingernails when I was very young. He would tell me don't tell anyone. I told everyone. I would write about it and pray always. I always felt as if I were doing something wrong.

As I grew older, he began groping my but and patting through my clothing and would smile and say don't tell no one or see how I would respond. I was very stubborn and angry. If he says don't. I would do the opposite. He would tell me to get on top of him and he would put his penis inside of me and ask me to put my mouth on his penis. I know this was wrong and constantly would tell my mother whom I thought would protect me and love me. Instead she chose money, man over me.

This one time my mom told me I wanted this man and didn't believe me. I was sure of what was wrong and right at this point and only in retrospect could identify what I was feeling. I didn't have a name for sex at that age, but I could feel it and know it was wrong deep in my heart. I felt wrong. He was an adult. He was a stepfather and did not love me. He treated me like a black sheep in the family an orphan. I felt separated from the real world. He even had two more children with my mother and the way they treated me
how the children treated me distantly. He treated his children with whatever they wanted and that was his

love to them and treated me like I was an adopted child with no protection and not loved.

I felt this problem my entirely life and surely mine and would feel disgusting and dirty. I didn't keep my secret closed. I kept telling my mother and everyone even when people would not want to hear or care. I knew and told the other family members even told his children my mother did not tell the I was ignored no one cared or loved me enough to help me. My stepfather didn't try to hide it and he didn't care he was always out with other women or young girls. He was a mailman, owned a business was very well known by the community.

He was physically and verbally abusive also his drinking and drugging and acted out and couldn't control himself.

This is a real story it happened to me. After continually telling my mother my stepfather keeps coming in my room late when you are asleep. My mother even put old school lock on the door. Finally, my mother and I discuss this molestation I am fourteen now.

We discussed a plan to catch him in my room, my mom "said" Pam the next time he comes in your room and touch you I want you to "scream real loud" until I get there, I said okay mama. ☐ ☐ The next day during the night he came in my room unlocked my door and put his fingers in my vagina with his long fingernails and I "screamed rea stepfather keeps coming in my room late when you are asleep.

My mother even put old school lock on the door. Finally, my mother and I discuss this molestation I am fourteen now. We discuss a plan to catch him in my room, my mom "said" Pam the next time he comes in your room and touch you I want you to "scream real loud" until I get there, I said okay mama. ☐ ☐ The next day during the night he came in my room unlocked my door and put his fingers in my vagina with his long fingernails and I "screamed real loud".

My mother heard me in my room there "he stands" and she saw blood on his long fingernails. I said mama, what are you going to do now? She asked him, why did you do this to my baby? That was all she did I left them both, it was time for me to go to middle school. As, I pass them by I heard him answer her saying; Margaret I didn't know what I was doing, and don't know why I did this. I did not return home from school that day. I tried to reach out to a family member to let them know what happened it was like talking to a wall. I knew this was true and he was caught like it was planned.

I was hard pressed on every side, but not crushed; perplexed, but not in despair; but not abandoned; struck down, but not destroyed. In 2004, My mother became ill before she died; she said
Pam I am so sorry for destroying your life of the choices I've made. I said mama I've forgave you all. I could see the peace from God on her face before she died. In 2005, I was asked by my sister to visit her father, which was my stepfather who molested me before he died.

I went to visit him, he did not say I'm sorry for what he did to me or asked for forgiveness. I hope he asked God for forgiveness. While visiting my biological father as an adult before he died I shared with him about the molestation. My dad loved me and showed me love. He immediately asked me; Pam what do you want me to do about him molesting you? My dad said; do you want me to kill him? I answered, no daddy let god take care of him because, I want to have you anymore.

God took care of it. I've told my story and did not tell it for pity. Because if you get pity you will undermined your prosperity. I tell it like a testimony. Not what's happening to you because life doesn't happen to you! You happen to life! Along time ago, I decided I would never be a poor copy of someone else when god made the original. Were you abused? Did you speak your truth, and no one believed you? Did you speak your truth and experience the pain?

If you were abused and someone, anyone didn't believe you, know that I do. I stand with you and for you in the way I can. Speaking the truth after being abused takes incredible courage and strength. I am proud of you. My story can be your story. #It's on Us. I am a survivor. You are a survivor. If you have been abused or are currently a victim of abuse and have not yet spoken out. I urge you to reach toward a safe person and speak your truth. You are strong and courageous and deserve to live an abuse free life. Stand with me, no longer a victim but a survivor. #It's on Us Start today and make a new ending. In Conclusion, my love of writing God picked out for me. Each gift of writing is unique. I have considered the ability to write well and a special gift.

2   PURPOSES OF LIFE
Writing I don't have to worry. It's working for me. I found my purpose of life God picked out for me. My love of writing, I have considered the ability to write well and a special gift. Purpose of writers often have more than one purpose for writing. Writing has a purpose, spoken conversations, writers join written conversations for purposes which effect the roles they adopt? Writers hoping to position are shaped by needs, interests, and backgrounds.

Just as writers have purposes, so do readers. Among other purposes, readers often want to learn about a subject, assess or evaluate ideas and arguments, or understand opposing perspectives. And like writers' purposes readers' purposes are strongly affected by their own needs, interests, and backgrounds. In Conclusion, my purpose of writing and love of writing God picked out for me builds on the work of others one of the most important ways persuade or convince their readers, for example, to take on the role of advocate, while those hoping to inform readers take on the role of reporter.

Writers purposes for joining conversation are shaped by needs, interests, and backgrounds. Just as writers have purposes, so do readers. Among other purposes, readers often want to learn about a subject, assess or evaluate ideas and arguments, or understand opposing perspectives.

And like writers' purposes readers' purposes are strongly affected by their own needs, interests, and backgrounds. ☐ ☐ In Conclusion, my purpose of writing and love of writing God picked out for me builds on the work of others one of the most important ways in
which writing situations resemble spoken conversations
people take turns sharing their ideas. ☐ ☐ ☐

3 MY LOVE OF WRITING GOD PICKED OUT FOR ME "LOVE IS LOVE'

Writing I don't have to worry it's working for me. I love writing what god picked out for me. Love what matters, what real love is all about.
Often, I feel love matters! What real love is all about? Often, we talk of all the things that we love, when truly, I feel what we mean is that sometimes, we mean is that we really like them. I feel this will help us to be mindful of the casual way to tend to use our

words, as well as a reminder to express our love to the people who mean the most in our lives. ☐ ☐ Loving God, loving others.

Our love for one another will prove to the world. This reminds me of how some can see god in us before personally recognizing reality ourselves. But how? For we don't receive a badge or jacket proclaiming to the world that we're Jesus disciples when we become believers in him. Some choose to make this identification based on whether a person goes to church or not, but we all know it's not that easy.

It could be quite difficult to identify whether someone is a true disciple of Christ. But in John 13, Jesus reveals how even without any kind of outward sign we can identify someone as a true believer: by the way we love one another.

Jesus said, "I am giving you a new commandment: Love each other. Just as I have loved you, you should love each other. This shouldn't surprise us, given how love is to our faith in him. Consider that love is the greatest commandment (Matthew 22:37-38) and the fulfillment of the entire Law (Romans 13:8). Love is also the evidence that Christ is Lord over our lives. Our love for one another will prove to the world that you are my disciples, the Savior declared (John 13:35). Our love for one another truly reveals our love for God. Love is love. Compassion literally means to "suffer with someone".

Our ability to feel others pain may be lacking until we find ourselves suffering through our own pain. We can easily live selfishly-desiring to be kept from hardship. Self-love is an effect of the fall, then we must understand what Jesus meant when he identified loving ourselves as the key to compassion), (brotherly love) or even (family affection), He commands us to live out God's agape love, and Agape love is giving, not getting. Jesus showed us great compassion as he gave his life for us. Through the Power of the holy Spirit, may we do less for others (Luke 10:27). Love can be our legacy as we reflect God, for he is love ".

For this is real love-not that we he God, but that he loved us. Kind and compassionate, caring and serving those qualities loving others (Romans 13:8-10). Not referring to (passion), (brotherly love) or even (family affection), He commands us to live out God's agape love, and Agape love is giving, not getting. Jesus showed us great compassion as he gave his life for us. Through the Power of the holy Spirit, may we do less for others (Luke 10:27). Love can be our legacy as we reflect God, for he is love ".

And this is real love-not that we he God, but that he loved us. Kind and compassionate, caring and serving those qualities mark the heart of a person who "lives like Jesus. May we also give up our lives for others as he works in and through us! Full of the fruit of the Spirit; love, joy, peace, patience, kindness, and more (Galatians 5:22-23). ☐ ☐ Dear Lord, Thank You for the unique way that you have gifted me. Help me to use my gifts faithfully to serve you and others, each person is a unique expression of God's loving design. ☐

☐ In Conclusion, my love of writing god picked out for me. Each gift of writing is unique have considered the ability to write well and a special gift. ☐ ☐ ☐ ☐ ☐

4 MY DREAM OF WRITING CONVERSATIONS ALLOW YOU TO ADOPT A ROLE

My Dream of writing God picked out for me deserves to be honored just as Dr. Martin Luther King Jr legacy today. I honor Dr. Martin Luther King by living his dream. I will write and pray on Dr. Martin Luther King's day as he always said, "I HAVE A DREAM". If I can't fly, then I will run, walk, If I can't walk, crawl, but whatever I do I will keep moving. Our dreams are gifts from God. Faith is taking the first step even when you don't see the whole staircase and don't settle for anything less! Start today, each gift is unique. I have considered the ability to write well as a special dream gift from God and honoring my dream of writing.

In spoken conversations, we often take on roles. A speaker might explain something to someone else, in a sense becoming a guide through the conversation. Another speaker might advance an argument, taking the role of an advocate for a position. These roles shift and change as the conversation moves along. Depending on the flow of the conversation, a person who explained something at one point in the conversation might make an argument later.   A similar form of role-playing and shifting takes place in written conversation. The roles writers take on reflect my purpose, my understanding of reading, and the types of documents I plan to write. In written conversation, what I write and read communication with one another.   Writing has a purpose more than writing a document, learn about a topic or improve skills, and writing as much for myself and readers. My purpose for writing conversation are needs, interests and backgrounds. I write using the gift of God picked out for me. Each gift of writing is unique. I have considered the ability to write well and a special gift. Taking the first step even when I don't see the whole staircase and don't settle for anything less!   Being a writer is closer too possible than you might have believed. Right in front of me all the time.

5 READING HAVE PURPOSES, NEEDS, INTERESTS, KNOWLEDGE AND BACKGROUNDS

Just as I write God picked out for me. Writers have purposes, so do readers. Among other purposes, readers often learn about a subject, assess or evaluate less ideas and arguments or understand opposing perspectives. And like writers' purposes, readers' purposes are strongly affected by our own, interest, and backgrounds.

George, my father for example, were driven by his awareness of the challenges faced by friends and family members who had served in the military. His readers were probably drawn to his post by similar personal experiences-knowing unemployed veterans, working in green jobs themselves, living in a region with many unemployed veterans, or simply having read an article or having heard a radio report about the issue.

   As writers craft their contributions to a written conversation, I would ask what readers are likely to be. I would reflect on readers are likely to be. I would reflect on readers' values and beliefs, determine what readers are likely to know about a subject, and consider readers' likely experiences- if any with the subject. And what readers might be interested in knowing. I would ask why potential readers would want to read my document-and what might cause readers to stop reading. I try to understand and connect with readers.

   I believe one of the most important ways in which writing situations resemble spoken conversations is reliance on taking turns. In spoken conversations-at least in those that are productive-people take turns sharing their ideas. To move the conversation forward, speakers build on what has been said, often referring to specific ideas or arguments and identifying the speakers who raised them. They show respect for the contributions made by others and help speakers align themselves with or distance themselves from other members of the conversation.

Even when writers do refer directly to other sources, writers are likely to influence thinking about a subject to a conversation that we've read, heard, seen, and experienced will shape your thinking about the subject by doing so, these sources will affect the information, ideas, and arguments in a document. Writers builds on the work of others. Most importantly in ways which writing situations resemble spoken conversations is reliance on taking turns. My purpose of writing conversation are needs, interests and backgrounds.

I write using the gift of writing is unique. I have considered he ability to write well and a special gift. Taking the first step even when I don't see the whole staircase and don't settle for anything less! Being a writer is closer too possible than you might have believed. Right in front of me all the time. When I can't see is that right over the next hill is something amazing, a new level.

6 WRITING CONVERSATIONS HELP YOU SHARE IDEAS AND ARGUMENTS

I write using the gift God picked out for me. Each gift of writing is unique. I have considered the ability to write well and a special gift. Much like a spoken conversation, a written conversation involves an exchange of words, however, the people engaged in the conversation communicate through written documents. Just as I listen to what's being said before contributing to a conversation most writers begin the process of writing about a topic by reading.   Among writers and readers becomes a circular process in which the information, ideas, and arguments shared through documents lead to the creation of new documents.

6   ATTRACTIONS

When somebody see something in you that you don't see in yourself the way they look at you, you long to see them look at you.

If you could only see in yourself what you are so fascinated what other people are seeing in you will begin to discover through your own eyes the gift that God has in you see ultimately it is not so important what you see, when you look at me, I'll a rise or fall over what I see when I look at me.

The bible says we were in our sights as grasshoppers and so were we in their sights, that it means if I see myself as a grasshopper, if I see myself as a giant killer ultimately other people will see me as a giant killer, if I see myself as a survivor, other people will see me as a survivor, if I see myself as valuable, other people will see me as valuable, and they will start saying something like that person I didn't think that person was so much at first but, you know they kind of grow on me all of a sudden they see your confidence, your self-esteem, your tenacity.

How you feel about you. You should believe there is something inside of you so valuable that anybody who rejects you has robbed themselves. You must feel like that leaving me would be a deficit that to lose me would be bankrupt. You must feel like that inside yourself.

You search ends when you look into your bible you are fearlessly and marvelously made you are created in Christ Jesus under good works that you are created in the lifeless and image of God you have treasure in you haven't even touched yet, things in you , you haven't even done yet, you don't know if you can fly a helicopter, you don't know if yet still checking me out.

   You are so special. There will never be another you. You ever had someone to die that you cared about you included they are not there look for them in other people eventually, you must conclude.

Occasionally, you run into people who remind you of them, but they are not there. You understand you are one of a kind. When I'm gone that's, it you will never replace. There'll never be another me in the world nowhere in the deepest part you can ski.

You don't need somebody to make you feel special. You are special. I got talents I haven't explored of Africa, in the tips of Russia the peaks of Paris. You're never find another me.

When God made, me he broke the gold, they can have my clothes and it won't be me do you know that about you? I'm talking about knowing who you are, thanking god for you, thanking god for what he gave you.

Why would you need a creature when you have a creator? Consider writing I have always thought about writing a book. I urge you to consider the desires of your heart. It provides an opportunity to share your expertise. It provides an opportunity to establish authority. It provides an opportunity to differentiate yourself. It provides an opportunity to expand your market. It provides an opportunity to launch a business. Whether you realize it or not, you are an expert.

I write using the gift God picked out for me. Each gift of writing is unique. I have considered the ability to write well and a special gift. Being a writer is closer too possible than you might have believed. I hope you enjoyed my writing and very grateful. Thank You!

8 Faith

The Lord is my light and my salvation whom I shall fear? The Lord is the stronghold of my life of whom I shall be afraid? When evil men advance against me to devour my flesh, when my enemies and my foes attack me, they will stumble and fall.

Though an army besiege me, my heart will not fear, though war break out against me, even then will I be confident.

One thing, I ask of the Lord all the days of my life, to gaze upon the beauty of the Lord and to seek him in his temple. For in the day of trouble he will keep me safe in his dwelling; He will hide me in the shelter of his tabernacle and set me upon a rock, then my head will be exalted above the enemies who surround me, at his tabernacle will I sacrifice with shouts of joy; I will sing and make music to the Lord.

Hear my voice when I call, O Lord; be merciful to me and answer me. My heart says of you, "Seek his face! Your face, Lord, I will seek. Do not reject me or forsake me, O God my Savior, though my father and mother forsake me, the Lord will receive me.

Teach me your way, O Lord; lead me in a straight path because of my oppressors, do not turn me over to the desire of my foes, for false witnesses' revolt against me, breathing out violence.

I am confident of this; I will see the goodness of the Lord in the land of the living. Wait for the Lord; be strong and take heart and wait for the Lord.

God planned something better. The fulfillment for them, as for us, is in Christ who is the resurrection and the life. (Jon 11:25-26). Only together with us would they be made perfect. All persons of faith who had gone before focused their faith on God and his promises. The fulfillment of Gods promises to them has now come in Jesus Christ, and their redemption too is now complete in him.

9 God's Promise to Abraham

The Lord said to Abraham, "Leave your country, your people and your father's household" and go to the land I will show you. I will make you into a great nation and I will bless you. I will make your name great, and you will be a blessing. I will bless those who bless you, and whoever curses you I will curse, and all peoples on earth will be blessed through you. (Gen. 12:4).

Abraham is the father to all who believe faith and God's promises and God's graciously responds to faith by crediting righteousness to one who believes. (Gen. 15:6). When Abraham was ninety-nine years old, the Lord appeared to him and said, "I am God Almighty". Walk before me and be blameless. I will confirm my covenant between me and you and will greatly increase your numbers. God appears to Abraham to reaffirm his promises.

But he also makes it clear that if Abraham is to receive covenanted benefits, he must live out "the obedience that comes from faith". To that end he calls on Abraham to make with him a covenanted commitment of loyal to obedience. (Gen. 17:1-27). Then God said take your son, your only son, Isaac, whom you love and go to the region of Moriah, sacrifice him there as a burnt offering on one of the mountains I will tell you about. (Gen.22:2-12).

When they reached the place, God had told him about, Abraham built an altar there and arranged the wood on it. He bound his son Isaac and laid him on the altar, on top of the wood.
Then he reached out his hand and took the knife to slay his son. But the angel of the Lord called out to him from heaven, "Abraham! Abraham! Here I am, he replied. Do not lay a hand on the boy, he said. Do not do anything to him. Now I know that you fear God, because you have not withheld from me your son, your only son. 10 Tests and Trials the Lord is with us always while adverse circumstances come out with a test.

"These trials will show that our faith is genuine. It is being tested as fire tests and purifies gold". (1Peter 1:7 a NLT) The Bible repeatedly says that God has promised to meet your needs: "And my God will meet all your needs per the riches of his glory in Christ Jesus (Philippians 4:19 NIV).

But the Bible also tells us that with every promise there is a condition. One of the conditions for this promise is that you should trust him. The more you trust God, the more God can meet needs in your life. When you go through them, you can know that it is an opportunity for you to develop your faith, so you can trust God more. I feel the Pressure Test asks a question, "How will I or you handle stress?" Will you depend on God? Psalm 50:15 says, "Call on me in the day of trouble; I will deliver you, and you will honor me".

God often uses people in your life to test and develop your faith. How we handle disappointment?" Life is often disappointing. Careers, marriages, and even plans don't turn out the way we planned them. But the most disappointing thing in life is people. Why? We get disappointed by people because we expect them to meet a need that only God himself can meet. This is a test!

Jeremiah 17:7 says, "Blessed are those who trust in the Lord whose confidence is in him. 11 Strong One who eats everything must not look down on him who does not, and the man who does, for God has accepted them. Be strong and do not fear. Words of encouragement. God will keep you strong to the end. Be strong and courageous, and do the work, do not be afraid or discouraged, for the Lord God, our God is with you.

God will not fail you or forsake you until the work for the service of the temple of the Lord is finished. Consider writing I have always thought about writing a book. I urge you to consider the desires of your heart.

It provides an opportunity to establish authority. It provides an opportunity to differentiate yourself. It provides an opportunity to expand your market. It provides an opportunity to launch a business. Whether you realize it or not, you are an expert.

I write using the gift God picked out for me. Each gift of writing is unique. I have considered the ability to write well and a special gift. Being a writer is closer too possible than you might have believed. I hope you've enjoyed my writing and very grateful. Thank You!

One of the Ten Commandments Honor your father and mother. God starts with the family because he created it. Honor your father and mother before a word is spoken about how to treat others. Few things in life can give us as much pleasure or pain! I am a living proof that no matter what we go through in life we all have the strength to get through it and past it if we allow ourselves to.

Don't be ashamed of your story it will inspire others. However, like all bad experiences, it is always possible to turn any experience into good by developing compassion and empathy for others who have been through all experiences. When I turn a negative experience into a tool that brings meaning into my life and others.

Forgiveness

As those who have been chosen of God, holy and beloved, put on a heart of compassion...bearing one another, forgiving each other, whosoever has a complaint against anyone just as the Lord forgave you, so also should you. Col3:12-13.

Unforgiveness holds us hostage, and when we find ourselves prisoners of what someone else has done to us or perhaps what we have done to ourselves. Forgiveness isn't necessarily the reconciliation of the relationship. Forgiveness is our choice to release a person from obligation for a wrong committed against us. God says to forgive one another because he paid the greater price the price of our sin debt-with his own son.

Loving god, loving others is the greatest commandment. Jesus showed us great compassion as he gave his life for us.

Dear Lord, Thank You for the unique way that you gifted me. Help me to use my gifts faithfully to serve you and others, each person is a unique expression of God's loving design.

I self-published my last book Overcoming Obstacles Survivor now you can read Overcoming Obstacles Family.

I am a living proof that no matter what we go through in life we all have the strength to get through it and past it if we allow ourselves to. Don't be ashamed of your story it will inspire others. However, like all bad experiences, it is always possible to turn any experiences. When I turn a negative experience into a tool that brings meaning into my life and others.

13 LOVE, FAMILY AND FORGIVENESS

I am a living proof that no matter what we go through in life we all have the strength to get through it and past it if we allow ourselves to. Don't be ashamed of your story it will inspire others. However, like all bad experiences, it is always possible to turn any experience into good by developing compassion and empathy for others who have been through all experiences. When I turn a negative experience into a tool that brings meaning into my life and others.

My Father, was a 'Veteran', United States Captain Corporal Marines Military "PVT Air Force".
It was February 13, 2017 I received a message concerning a legal matter of property heirs and did not know of the inheritance for me an only child of my dad. My father's parents which are my grandparents whom died without leaving a written will and left no

unpaid estate or inheritance taxes, debts that were unpaid. They owned two lots of real property I now have learned my signature was forged and/or in the presence of a notary.

One of my dreams owning property this was exciting just to know I inherited a blessing. My signature was signed without my consent. My situation goes past the point of what to do about my forged signature and runs into some legal and possibly law enforcement issues.

What does Family Mean to Me?

There are things in life we simply do not have a choice about. These include birth, death, taxes and, of course, the group of people we are permanently associated with. From the moment of conception, we are placed by fate with individuals who will help shape our entire lives… our family.
But through every argument, every "inconsiderate" decision my parents made and every time I'd "push my limits," I'm still forced to admit the truth: without my family, I wouldn't be the person I am today.

A deeper look to consider my family life shows where peculiarity originates: like me, my family has never been the "normal kind". My mom is a Houstonian, and my dad, and grandfather was a veteran. My mother's, mom gave her to another family to raise her in "Los Angeles California," until she was the age of 10 years old. My grandmother had six children, my mother was the only one she gave away to that family.

My family is the kind that sticks out like a conventional family; While t's hard for me to admit it, a lot of my self-proclaimed "uniqueness" is probably inspired by my parents. The ideal of being "different' and standing out. I never form an opinion based on what others think or tell me and I strongly value these qualities in the people I choose to spend time with.

Family means the people who accept you no matter who you are where there's no hatred or judgement. The love of a family should be unconditional, and everyone should try their best to provide all they can for the people in their family, emotionally and financially. Family are the people that everyone deserves.

14 WHAT THE BIBLE SAY ABOUT FAVORITISM

Favoritism is partiality or bias. To show favoritism is to give preference to one person over others with equal claims. It is like discrimination and may be based on conditions such as social class, wealth, clothing, actions, etc. What the Bible say about favoritism Ephesians 6:9 says, "There is no favoritism with him. Colossians 3:25 teaches God's fairness in judgement: Anyone who does wrong will be repaid for his wrong, and there is no favoritism.

The Bible is clear that favoritism is not God's will for our lives. First, favoritism is incongruent with God's character: "God does not show favoritism" (Romans 2:11). All are equal before Him. Ephesians 6:9 says, "There is no favoritism with him. "Colossians 3:25 teaches God's fairness in judgement: Anyone who does wrong, will be paid for his wrong, and here is no favoritism.

Second, the bible teaches Christians are not to show favoritism: "My brothers as believers in our glorious Lord Jesus Christ, don't show favoritism." (James2:1) The context concerns the treatment of rich and poor in the church. James points out that treating someone differently based on his financial status or how he is dressed is wrong.

Leviticus 19:15 teaches, do not per vert justice; do not show partiality to the poor or favoritism to the great, but judge your neighbor fairly. Exodus 23:31 likewise commands, "Do not show favoritism to a poor man in his lawsuit." Justice should be blind and both rich and poor should be treated equally before the law.

Third, the Bible calls favoritism sin: "If you really keep the royal law found in scripture, "Love your neighbor as yourself, "you are doing right. But if you show favoritism, you sin and are convicted by the "laws as lawbreakers" (James 2:8-9.) Favoritism is a serious offense against God's call to love one's neighbor as oneself.

Fourth, church leaders are especially charged not to show favoritism Paul commanded Timothy a young church leader in the sight of God and Christ.

Jesus and the elect angels, to keep these instructions without partiality, and to do nothing out of favoritism (1Timothy 5:21.) Fifth, it is difficult to avoid showing favoritism, even Christ's followers struggled with bias against people different from them. When the apostle Peter was first called to minister to non-Jewish people, he was reluctant. He later admitted, "I now realize how true it is that God does not show favoritism but accepts men from every nation who fear him and do what is right."

(Acts 10:34). The fact that James specifically addresses the sin of favoritism implies that this was a frequent problem within the early church. Favoritism is a problem and we still deal with. Favoritism and partiality are not from God, and Christians are called to love.

As, humans, we tend to form judgements based on selfish, personal criteria rather than seeing others as God sees them. May we grow in the grace and knowledge of our Lord and Savior Jesus Christ and follow his example of treating every person with God's love. (John 3:16). Dear Lord, Thank You for the unique way that you have gifted me. Help me to use my gifts faithfully to serve you and others each person is a unique expression of God's loving design.

15 THE PARENTING PERILS OF FAVORITISM

It started with an unusual pregnancy, after many years, God granted Isaac and Rebekah's fervent request for a child. (Genesis 25: 19-34.) Abraham became the father of Isaac, Isaac as forty years old, when he married Rebekah daughter of Bethel the Aramean from Padden Aram and sister of Laban the Aramean. Isaac prayed to the Lord on behalf of his wife, because she was barren.

The Lord answered his prayer, and his wife Rebekah became pregnant. The babies jest led each other within her and she said. "Why is this happening to me? So, she went to inquire of the Lord." The Lord said to her, two nations are in your womb and two peoples from within you will be separated; one people will be stronger than the other, and the older will serve the younger.

When the time came for her to give birth, there were twin boys in her womb. The first to come out was red, and his whole body was like a hairy garment, so they named him Esau. After this, his brother came out, with his hand grasping Esau's heel; so, he was named Jacob. Isaac was sixty years old when Rebekah gave birth to them. The boys grew up, and Esau became a skilled hunter, a man of the country, while Jacob was a quiet man, staying among the tents.

Isaac, who had taste for wild game, loved Esau, but Rebekah loved Jacob. Once when Jacob was cooing some stew, Esau came in from the open country, furnished, He said to Jacob, "Quick, let me have some of that red stew! "I'm farnished." (That is why he was called Edom,") Esau lost his blessing. Jacob replied, "First sell me your birthright." Look, I am about to die, "Esau said; "What good is the birthright to me? But, Jacob said, "Swear to me first" So he swore an oath to him, selling his birthright to Jacob.

"You give up your blessings." Then Jacob gave Esau some bread and some lentil stew. He ate and drank and then got up and left. So, Esau despised his birthright, in so doing he proved himself to be "godless (Hebrews 12:16). See that no one is sexually immoral, or is godless like Esau, who for a single meal sold his inheritance rights as the oldest son. Afterward, as you know, when he wanted to inherit this blessing, he was rejected.

He could bring about no change of mind though he sought the blessing with tears.
Godless like Esau he had no appreciation for true values he despised his birthright by valuing food for

his stomach more highly than his birthright. He was rejected because he only regretted his loss and did not repent of his sin.

His sorrow was not "godly sorrow" that brings repentance that leads to salvation but "worldly sorrow" that brings death (2Corinthians 7:10) could bring about no change of mind. Could not undo what he had done Blessing of the firstborn. Compromising their faith to gain relief from persecution. But to trade their spiritual birthright for temporary ease in this world would deprive them of Christ's blessing, with tears, not tears of repentance.

16 SECRETS

When you keep a secret, you live in fear betraying yourself, betraying others. To protect people, fear of consequences, to cover up poor choices, can't correct the problem. Sin is at the root of all our problems doesn't mean your sins, it does mean sin is at the root of our problems. Whether there is personal, psychological, spiritual, environmental, family, physical sin is at the root of our problem. Psalm 44:21 says would not God have discovered it, since he knows the secrets of the heart? Romans 2:16 This will take place on the day when God will judge men's secrets through Jesus Christ.

1 Corinthians 14:25 says and the secrets of his heart will be laid bare. So, he will fall and worship God, exclaiming," God is really among you." Revelations 2:24 Now I say to the rest of you in Thyatira, to you who do not hold to her teaching and have not learned Satan's so-called deep secrets (I will not impose any other burden on you.): Deuteronomy 29:29 says the things belong to the Lord our God, but the things revealed belong to us and to our children forever, that we may follow all the words of this law.

Judge 16:6 So Delilah said to Sampson, "Tell me the secret of your great strength and how you can be told up and subdued. Psalm 90:8 You have set our iniquities before you, our secret sin in the light of your presence. Psalm 139:15 My frame was not hidden from you when I was made in the secret place. When I was woven together in the depths of the earth.

Peter 2:1 But there were also false prophets among the people, just as there will be false teachers among you. They will secretly introduce destructive heresies even denying the sovereign Lord who bought them bringing swift destruction on themselves. Proverbs 11:13 A gossip betrays a confidence, but a trustworthy man keeps a secret. Jeremiah 23:24 Can anyone hide in secret places so that I cannot see him?

Matthew 6:4 So that your giving may be in secret. Then your Father, who sees what is done in secret, will reward you. Mark 4:11 The secret of the Kingdom of God has been given to you. But to those on the outside everything is said in parables. 1 Corinthians 2:7 So then men ought to regard us as servants of Christ and as those entrusted with the secret things of God. 2Corinthians 4:2 Rather, we have renounced secret and shameful ways; we do not use deception, nor do we distort the word of God.

Ephesians 5:12 For it is shameful even to mention what the disobedient do in secret. Philippians 4:4 Do not be anxious about anything, but in everything, by prayer and petition with thanksgiving, present your requests to God, which transcends all understanding, will guard your hearts and your minds in Christ Jesus. Philippians 4:12 I know what it is to be in need and I know what it is to have plenty. I have learned the secret of being content in any and every situation, whether well fed or hungry, whether living in plenty or in want.

17 LOVE FROM THE INSIDE OUT

My vision has always been to help people, as a survivor, victim been abused. If you have been abused or currently a victim of abuse and have not yet spoken out. I urge you to reach toward a safe person and speak your truth. You too are strong and courageous and deserve to live an abuse free life. Stand with me, no longer a victim but a survivor.

My business is to pursue dreams of publishing my own books, achieve goals; idea of the future way helps me, help people improve and create a purpose that becomes my measurement for success. So, getting my book published February 8, 2017 has been one of strong and current vision connects with my passion and greatest potentials. While working on my books, I noticed the change starts from within me a real story of my life what happened to me. Success writings have focused on solutions to specific problems. This is known as the character ethic such as integrity, courage, justice, patience etc.

As I do the Lord's work the Holy Spirits is always the primary counselor and works powerfully, sovereignty through the word. Through scriptures that teaches to live a life of faith and obedience in response to saving grace. Through the scriptures the holy spirit comforts, rebukes, corrects, and trains in righteousness. In this way people of all ages and from various walks of life are healed; all kinds of personal, marriage and family problems are resolved, and God is glorified.

It is therefore essential for us to be "thoroughly equipped" with the scriptures prepared for "every excellent work." The better equipped we are the more effective we will be in helping others. It starts in the heart when we allow God to create within us a clean heart. God sees inside of our heart we do not judge others, because only God sees into a person's heart.

It's always better not to judge others and instead to try to understand their thoughts and feelings of others, to get to know them the way God knows them. People are like books, you should look inside to know what is there.

Though inside out moved young and old to look inside our own minds.
Joy, sadness, anger, fear, and disgust has some deep things to say about the nature of our emotions. They are conveyed strongly enough to provide a foundation discussion among children and adults alike. Happiness is not just about joy I have learned that there is much, much more to being happy than boundless positively. Happiness is: the experience of joy, contentment, or positive well-being, combined with a sense that one's life is good, meaningful, and worthwhile."

People who experience "emo diversity", a life containing a balance of different emotions is good for you. Both positive and negative emotions, have better mental health. For example, I allowed myself to feel sadness, as a victim of abuse in addition to fear and anger. I had been abused and the idea of running away from home; as a result, I decided not to go through with the plan.

This choice reunites me with my family, giving a deeper sense of happiness and contentment in the comfort I sometimes received from my parents, even though it was mixed with sadness and fear. Joy instead of "Happiness." Ultimately, joy was just one element of happiness, and happiness can be tinged with other emotions, even including sadness. What I didn't do was force happiness don't try to force happiness, I felt an old familiar frustration when told to be a happy girl, while the family adjusts to a stressful life.

As a child, my parents got similar messages and used to think something was wrong with me if I wasn't happy all the time. It was being molested a five-year-old until fourteen years old. The research suggests that making happiness an explicit goal in life can make you miserable. Thank god, more people strive for happiness the greater the chance that they'll set very high standards of happiness for themselves and feel disappointed and less happy when they're not able to meet these standards all the time.

So, it should come as no surprise that trying to force herself to be happy doesn't help to deal with the stresses and transitions in my life. In fact, not only did that strategy fail to bring me happiness, it also, seem to make me feel isolated and angry with my parents which made me want to run away from home. What's a more effective route to happiness for me and the rest of us importance of "prioritizing positivity" deliberately carving out ample time in life for experiences that we personally enjoy.

For Pamela, a long time ago, I decided I would never be a poor copy of someone else when God made the original.

Were you abused? Did you speak your truth, and no one believed you? Did you speak your truth and experience the pain of even one person doubting you? If you were abused and someone, anyone didn't believe you, know that I do. I stand with you and for you in the way I can.

Speaking the truth after being abused takes incredible courage and strength. I am proud of you. My story can be your story. # Its on Us. I am a Survivor. You should believe there is something inside of you so valuable that anybody who rejects you has robbed themselves. You must feel like that leaving me would be a deficit. That to lose me would be bankrupt.

You must feel like that inside yourself. You search ends when you consider your Bible you are fearlessly and marvelously made you are created in Christ Jesus under good works that you are created in lifeless and image of God you are treasure in you, you haven't even touched yet, things in you.

What's a more effective route to happiness for me and the rest of us importance of "prioritizing positivity" deliberately carving out ample time in life for experiences that we personally enjoy. For Pamela, along things in you, you haven't done yet, you don't know if you can ski. You don't need somebody to make you feel special. You are special. I have talents I haven't explored yet still checking me out.

18 SURVIVORS

If you have been abused or currently a victim of abuse and have not yet spoken out. I urge you to reach toward a safe person and speak your truth. You too are strong and courageous and deserve to live an abuse free life. Stand with me, no longer a victim but a survivor.

One of the distressing and utterly frustrating and despairing things that survivors of abuse discover as adults, is that some parents deny that anything ever happened. When confronted by my parent as an adult child, what my mom "said" was I don't know. Some parents would say their memory is wrong.

I can remember when it was natural to confront my mother about the abusive acts that happened during childhood.

Apparently, I as a survivor was seeking an apology, an affirmative statement admitting their wrong doing. This is what makes the discussion so filled with despair for so many survivors. The despair results not simply by the refusal of an apology, but the complete denial that anything happened. This is further exacerbated by the fact that family, neighbors and friends of the parents think their very "nice people" who would never do such a despicable thing as abuse a child.

When I published the story of my childhood a story that depicted family cruel and outlandish acts of abuse, there was a public outcry that this never could have happened. Later, the outcry vanished when the truth and accuracy of the story emerged for the public to see.

It is the responsibility of neighbors, family, friends, teachers and school officials to report suspected abuse to the authorities who will then investigate.

Do not play the "hear no evil, see no evil" game. Act on what you know or have good reason to suspect. #It's on Us. The healing began loving me inside and out teaching me and God changing me the transformative moment I have been waiting for have arrived. But because I know what it takes to heal mainly courage, love, and lots of time and managed to keep my soul.

19 HOW PARENTS CREATE SIBLING RIVALRY

Luke 12:52-56 Not Peace but Division From now on here will be five in one family divided against each other, three against two, and two against three. They will be divided, father against son and son against father, mother against daughter and daughter, against mother, mother in-law against daughter-in-law and daughter-in-law against mother-in-law.

How Parents Create Sibling Rivalry Narcissist is a person who is overly self-involved, and often vain and selfish. Someone concern with his or her interests. This is the only way I can describe narcissism relationships. Because narcissists are incredibly self-centered, they have precious little time to spend with their children.

In functional families, sibling rivalry naturally occurs and, with adequate parenting, ideally occurs and, with adequate parenting ideally turns into respect for each other as children mature. Siblings are encouraged to be close and love each other. This isn't the case in my family a constant comparison between siblings. I am the oldest of my sister and brother.

I long to feel the closeness I see my friends with their siblings. Sadly, siblings with narcissistic parents often sacrifice relationships with each other to compete for something that doesn't exist my parents unconditional love. At times, I would feel frustrated with myself or unworthy and inadequate and project those self-deprecating feelings onto my siblings as well. When you were taught from an early age to repress their feelings and that they don't matter.

Children are often put into shifting roles. First, the golden child, is the hero, the mother's other half, or their mirror. There are pros to this role, such as getting all the best stuff, the attention, and the ability to entertain the illusion you can do no wrong. Your accomplishment, no matter how minor, are celebrated fully.

However, it's not all sunshine and rainbows for the golden child. I have become enmeshed without narcissistic parents and grew up without any factual knowledge of boundaries or self-identity. In this spotlight was one whom the other siblings are ultimately the most jealous. Then there's the scapegoat. When you receive attention from your parents in this role it's of the negative variety. But, oh the relief in feeling you are at last beyond control.

That feeling was short-lived as a child because they significant effort to strip me of that control and tried as an adult, they did not have the power to do. When in the scapegoat role, you shoulder the blame, shame, and anger of the family. If something goes wrong, it's your fault. You are labeled as the "bad one", even if you don't fit into the category. The scapegoat role is that you often have a better concept of self and independence than does the golden child, which can help you later in life.

Finally, if you are the last child, the forgotten one that receives neither praise nor the blame, you may do your best to remain invisible and away from your parent's wrath. You sense it might be better to go unnoticed than to have to deal with the emotionally debilitating games your parents play with the other children.

Some parents intentionally triangulate and pit their children against one another. When I say triangulate it means three roles are being played. Where there is the villain, the victim, and the rescuer. The villain is the one who blames, disrespects, attacks, or criticizes the victim. In turn, this tempts the rescuer to defend the victim, which can move the rescuer into the villain into the victim's place.

The roles often switch and reverse. For example, the parents can start out as the villain and the scapegoat, as her victim. If you try to become your siblings' rescuer when your brother or sister is in the villain role, me instead become the villain in my mother's eyes for betraying her.

And she in turn, is now the victim of me and tempts my siblings to become the rescuer to gain my mother's positive attention. It is an exhausting emotional game, that never end. Some parents intentionally block bonding and encourage competition between siblings.

Other parents create vacuum of neglect where the children are left to prey upon each other for the emotional resources that are available in the family environment.

Families like this can feel like an emotional desert. The result of tactics like emotional abuse, lies, and neglect, however, ensures her children are always on their toes, working to earn her conditional love.

The negative feelings you have toward your siblings while growing up can carry on well into your adult life. My siblings are not close to each other due to the deep emotional scars animosity, they were programmed to feel towards each other by the narcissistic family environment.

I finally realize one or two of my siblings is unable to let go of the old system and actively keeps the rivalry going today, every day. He or she will then miss the value of having sister survivor, my brother or sister, who didn't want to understand what they endured.

As adult children competition between my siblings have decreased there is no realization by all parties that we were taught growing up is not how siblings need act towards each other.

There is no opportunity to create trust and bonding between adult siblings that was not possible as children caught in the destructive narcissistic pattern of parenting. Family that prays together stays together.

20 STRANGERS WE CALL FAMILY

Experiencing abuse is one of the most horrific, violent, confusing acts anyone can ever go through. Writing, thinking of it brings back the depths of so many violent and intense emotions. All I know is that it is incredibly a healing, strong and I can feel peace, real, and it is finished.

It took me a long time to allow myself to separate from its strangulating grip. Probably one of the most shocking aspects of sexual abuse is the identity of the abuser, because they are usually all those people we believe "could never" abuse. They are our brothers, fathers, uncles, cousins, family, friends, the guy next door.

This is something that begins within our very own circles, in our families amongst our neighbors. It is a sobering thought to realize that there are people I don't trust. And how frequent it is that they walk away scot-free, with their sick behavior. While the child who has been brutally invaded is accused and left to suffer.

There is no excuse for defending an abuser. Yes, maybe he is a nice person, a kind mother, or father, or the all-too familiar attempt at justification" they were abused themselves" but this is not an answer and in no way, changes the situation. The facts remain that they were an abuser.

    They are accountable for their actions. I was the one abused I will not be held guilty by family, and no one else. Love, was there anything left to love? Wait, what was love? "Love" betrayed me, love was just a mask for the sickness man is capable of. Why would I want to allow any aspect of "love" to enter my life? The strictness of how my mother had to ask my step-father if I could go to any activity and clean everything, I can remember some friends help me

    I felt he wanted to save me for himself. I was not allowed to go with friends, or classmates. Only, now do I see that my reasons were irrational and senseless, yet at the time I could not see beyond them. It leaves the responsibility to the parents to look but, for any warning signs, and be open with your daughters and sons about abuse and listen to them.

For many years, I have struggled to get beyond the experiences that have scarred me, but I know I would have never been able to get to this place without God. Psalm 40: 1-3 I waited patiently for the Lord he heard my cry. He lifted me out of the mud and mire. He set my feet on a rock and gave me a firm place to stand. "Thank You Father" for using me, and the "plan you have for my life" how you picked it out for me.

    I don't understand how parents can sleep at night knowing that they are actively feigning ignorance after their child has been abused. I can only begin to imagine the pain, it is really causing the parent, but ignoring it will not make it disappear, and will only aggravate the situation.

"The sooner its dealt with, the sooner everyone can move on. And a "child who has been abused" cannot be judged for his or her own self abusive behavior, because probably he or she doesn't understand it. I can, and most of all the power to create realities that are honest, meaningful and real. If you have been abused or currently a victim of abuse and have not yet spoken out.

    I urge you to reach toward a safe person and speak your truth. You too, are strong and courageous, and deserve to live an abuse free life. Stand with me, no longer a victim, but a survivor.

Phillipians3:13 Brothers, I do not consider myself yet to have taken hold of it. But one thing I do; Forgetting what is behind" and straining toward what is ahead, I press on toward the goal to win the prize for which God has called me heavenward in Christ Jesus.

Jeremiah29:11-12" For I know the plans" I have for you, declares the Lord, plans to prosper you and not to harm you, plans to give you hope and a future.

Then you will call upon me and come and pray to me, and I will bring you back from captivity. I will gather you from all the nations and places where I back to the place from which I carried you into exile.

Phillipians4:6-7 Do not be anxious about anything, but in everything, by prayer and petition, with thanksgiving, present your requests to God. And the peace of God, which transcends all understanding, will guard your hearts and your minds in Christ Jesus.

Phillipians4:11-13 I am not saying this because I am in need, for I have learned to be content whatever the circumstances, I know what it is to be in need, and I know what it is to have plenty. I have learned to be content whatever the circumstances, I know what it is to be in need, and I know what it is to have plenty. I have learned the secret of being content in any and every situation whether well fed or hungry, whether living in plenty or in want. I can do everything through him who gives me strength. Phillipians4:19 And my

God will meet all needs according to his glorious riches in Christ Jesus.

John19:30 "IT IS FINISHED"
Thank You Father for my "LOUD CRY"

    I write using the gift God picked out for me. Each gift of writing is unique. I have considered the ability to write well and a special gift. Being a writer is closer too possible than you might have believed. I hope you've enjoyed my writing and I am very grateful. Thank You!
_Pamela Renee' Knight

_Pamela Renee' Knight 1/28/2018

ABOUT THE AUTHOR

Knight, P. Renee' (2018)
Overcoming Obstacles My writing is God's gift to me. I figured out my purpose, figured out my passion, it leads me right into my purpose. My love of writing God picked out for me.